Gracefully Free

A Journey to Thriving After Divorce

Healing, Growth, and New Beginnings

Glendora Sealy

Dedication

To my incredible children—my greatest source of strength and joy.

Thank you for walking beside me through every chapter of this transition, for lifting me up on the days when the weight felt too heavy, and for celebrating each small victory along the way. Your encouragement, patience, and unconditional love gave me the courage to step into a new life after divorce with hope instead of fear.

I am deeply grateful for your understanding hearts, your gentle reminders to keep going, and the light you brought into moments when I needed it most. This book is not only a reflection of my journey but a testament to our shared resilience. You inspired me to rebuild, to dream boldly, and to believe that new beginnings are always possible.

This is for you with all my love and gratitude.

Acknowledgment

First and foremost, I give all honor and glory to God. It is only through His grace, His strength, and His unshakable love that I was able to rise from one of the most challenging seasons of my life. Every page of this book is a testimony of His healing power and His promise that beauty can truly come from broken places. God carried me when I felt weak, restored me when I felt lost, and reminded me that my story was not over.

To my precious children, thank you for standing with me through every chapter of this journey. Your love, your understanding, and your encouragement gave me the courage to keep pressing forward. You are my heart, my joy, and a daily reminder of God's blessings. I dedicate this book to you with deep love and gratitude.

To my counselors who uplifted me, and wrapped me in support. Thank you for being vessels of God's comfort. Your faith in me strengthened my own, and your presence helped me rebuild with confidence and peace.

To every reader who may be navigating the pain of divorce, I pray that this book speaks to your heart. May you feel God's nearness, may you trust His timing, and may you find hope in the new beginnings He is preparing for you.

With faith, gratitude, and love.

Contents

Introduction

Embracing Change and Thriving After Divorce

Divorce is one of life's most challenging transitions. It brings a whirlwind of emotions - grief, anger, confusion, relief, and sometimes even guilt. It's the end of a chapter, and with it comes a profound sense of loss. But while divorce marks the closing of one door, it also opens another - a door to rediscovery, growth, and transformation.

This book is not just about healing from divorce; it's about thriving beyond it. It's about shifting your focus from what was lost to what can be gained. Whether you are newly separated or have been divorced for years, this journey is about more than just surviving — it's about rebuilding a life that is fulfilling, joyful, and uniquely your own.

Thriving after divorce means reclaiming your sense of self, embracing new opportunities, and redefining happiness on your own terms. It means letting go of old narratives, fostering self-love, and building resilience. It is a chance to create a life that aligns with your deepest values and desires.

Throughout this book, we will explore how to navigate emotions, rebuild confidence, create a strong support system, and rediscover passions that may have been set aside. We will look at practical steps for financial independence, co-parenting strategies, and ways to cultivate new relationships—whether romantic, platonic, or the most important one of all: the relationship with yourself.

Divorce is not the end of your story. It's the beginning of a new chapter—one where you are the author of your own happiness. The pain you have experienced does not define you; what you do next does.

Let's embark on this journey together. Let's turn this transition into an opportunity for growth, empowerment, and a life filled with purpose and joy. You are not alone, and you are more capable than you realize.

Your new beginning starts now.

Chapter 01

The Emotional Journey

Divorce is a profound life event that can evoke a whirlwind of emotions. Understanding these emotional stages can empower you to navigate this journey with greater self-awareness and resilience.

The Stages of Grieving

Divorce, like other significant losses, often involves a grieving process. The emotions you experience may not follow a linear path, and it's normal to cycle through or revisit different stages.

Denial:

Denial acts as an emotional buffer, allowing you to gradually process the reality of the divorce. You might find yourself thinking, *"This can't be happening to me,"* or holding onto the hope of reconciliation. This stage provides temporary relief but can delay the acceptance of the situation.

Anger:

As reality sets in, anger can surface. You may direct this anger at your ex-partner, yourself, or the circumstances. Feelings of betrayal, injustice, or frustration are common. It's essential to acknowledge and express this anger in healthy ways, as suppressing it can lead to further emotional harm.

Bargaining:

Bargaining often involves reflecting on the past and imagining how things could have been different. Thoughts like, *"If only I had done this differently, we might still be together,"* are frequent in this stage. Bargaining can be a way to regain a sense of control but may also foster feelings of guilt or regret.

Depression:

The weight of loss can lead to periods of sadness and withdrawal. You may grieve the loss of shared dreams, companionship, and the life you once knew. While this stage is difficult, it is a critical part of healing, allowing you to confront and process deep-seated emotions.

Acceptance:

Acceptance doesn't mean you are "over" the divorce, but it signifies a recognition of your new reality. You begin to let go of past grievances, forgive yourself and your ex-partner, and look forward to building a new chapter in your life. Acceptance allows for personal growth and the possibility of finding joy again.

Coping with Emotional Waves

Everyone's journey is unique, and there's no set timeline for healing. Your coping ability can be influenced by factors such as:

Support System: Friends, family, or support groups can offer a sense of community and understanding.

Self-Care Practices: Engaging in activities that promote physical and emotional well-being, like exercise, journaling, or meditation.

Professional Help: Therapists or counselors specializing in divorce can provide tailored guidance and coping strategies.

Remember, experiencing these emotions is a normal part of the process. By understanding and accepting these feelings, you take the first step toward healing and rebuilding your life after divorce.

Chapter 02
Self-Care and Healing

Mental and Emotional Well-being

○ Self-care is an essential aspect of healing after divorce. It involves nurturing both the mind and body to regain emotional balance and inner peace. Below are some ways to prioritize mental and emotional well-being:

Daily Meditation for Mind and Soul

○ Practicing meditation daily can help calm the mind, reduce stress, and enhance emotional resilience. Guided meditation, simple reflection exercises, or deep breathing techniques can aid in processing emotions and fostering inner peace. Even just a few minutes of stillness each morning set a positive tone for the day.

Physical Exercise for Strength and Social Connection

○ Joining a gym or engaging in regular physical activity not only strengthens the body but also boosts mental well-being. Exercise releases endorphins, which can improve mood and reduce stress. Additionally, a gym or fitness class can provide opportunities to meet new people, fostering social connections that can be uplifting during challenging times. Walking outdoors is another great option, offering both physical benefits and a sense of distraction from negative emotions.

Journaling as a Tool for Healing

o Journaling is a powerful way to process emotions and gain clarity during the healing journey. Writing down thoughts, feelings, and reflections can provide a safe space for self-expression, allowing individuals to work through their emotions at their own pace. Journaling prompts such as "What am I grateful for today?" or "What lesson have I learned from this experience?" can help shift focus toward personal growth and resilience.

Embracing Daily Affirmations

o Positive affirmations can help reframe negative thoughts and boost self-esteem. Repeating affirmations like "I am strong and capable," "I deserve love and happiness," or "Each day, I grow stronger and wiser" can encourage a more optimistic outlook and enhance self-worth.

Creating Personal Boundaries

o Establishing personal boundaries is crucial in the healing process. Learning to say no, prioritizing self-care, and distancing oneself from toxic relationships or negative influences can promote emotional well-being. Setting boundaries allows individuals to focus on their needs and cultivate healthier relationships moving forward.

Physical Health and Wellness

Nutrition for Optimal Healing

○ Eating a balanced diet plays a vital role in overall well-being. Consuming a variety of foods rich in carbohydrates, proteins, vitamins, and minerals can provide the necessary energy and nutrients to support both physical and emotional recovery. Hydration is also essential; drinking plenty of water and herbal teas can help flush out toxins and maintain bodily functions.

Quality Sleep for Restoration

○ Sleep is an essential component of the healing process. A well-rested body and mind can better cope with stress and emotional turmoil. Developing a nighttime routine, such as avoiding screens before bed, practicing relaxation techniques, and maintaining a consistent sleep schedule, can improve sleep quality.

The Power of Massage and Relaxation

○ A simple massage can aid in relaxation by relieving tension, improving circulation, and reducing stress levels. Whether through professional massage therapy or self-massage techniques, incorporating relaxation practices can promote a sense of calm and well-being.

○ By focusing on self-care and healing, individuals can regain a sense of balance, rebuild their confidence, and create a fulfilling life after divorce. Prioritizing mental, emotional, and physical health is a crucial step toward embracing a new chapter with strength and positivity.

Chapter 03
Parenting after Divorce

Single Parenting Strategies

Parenting after divorce comes with unique challenges, but with the right strategies, it can be a fulfilling and positive experience for both you and your children. Here are some key approaches to help navigate this journey:

1. Time Management and Organization

Balancing work, household responsibilities, and parenting can be overwhelming. Developing a structured routine can provide stability for both you and your children.

- Create a daily and weekly schedule – This includes school, extracurricular activities, mealtimes, and bedtime routines.

- Set priorities – Focus on the most important tasks and let go of perfection.

- Use planners or digital apps – Tools like shared calendars (Google Calendar, Cozi) can help coordinate schedules, especially if co-parenting.

2. Building a Support System

Raising children alone does not mean you have to do it all by yourself. Having a strong support system is crucial.

- Reach out to family and friends – Loved ones can offer emotional support or help with childcare.

- Join single-parent support groups – Connecting with others in similar situations can provide encouragement and advice.

- Engage with your community – Local organizations, churches, or parenting groups can be valuable resources.

3. Co-Parenting Cooperation

If both parents are involved in the child's life, maintaining a cooperative co-parenting relationship can make things smoother.

- Keep communication child-focused – Discuss schedules, school matters, and important decisions without letting personal conflicts interfere.

- Be flexible but set boundaries – Adapt when necessary, but also establish consistent guidelines.

- Encourage the child's relationship with the other parent – Unless there are safety concerns, children benefit from having both parents actively involved.

4. Financial Management

Being financially independent after divorce can be challenging. Planning ahead can ease the burden.

- Create a realistic budget – Account for expenses like child-care, education, and medical needs.

- Seek financial assistance if needed – Government programs, grants, or child support can provide additional help.

- Teach children about financial responsibility – As they grow, involve them in basic budgeting discussions.

5. Self-Care for Single Parents

Taking care of yourself allows you to be the best parent for your children.

- Prioritize your mental and physical well-being – Exercise, eat well, and get enough rest.

- Make time for hobbies and social activities – You deserve a fulfilling life beyond parenting.

- Seek professional support if needed – Therapy or counsel-ing can help manage stress and emotions.

By implementing these strategies, single parents can create a nur-turing and stable environment for their children, while also main-taining their own well-being.

Chapter 04

Financial Independence

Rebuilding Your Finances

Divorce brings not just emotional adjustments but also financial changes. As a newly single individual, it is crucial to develop new financial skills and take proactive steps to ensure financial stability. Managing money effectively requires learning how to budget, make independent financial decisions, and plan for the future.

One of the first steps in rebuilding finances post-divorce is understanding your new financial reality. This involves assessing your income, expenses, assets, and debts. Creating a detailed budget will help you track your spending and ensure that you live within your means. Budgeting tools and apps can assist in managing finances efficiently.

Developing a Financial Plan

A solid financial plan provides a roadmap for your future. Key aspects include:

- **Setting Financial Goals**: Identify short-term and long-term financial objectives, such as saving for emergencies, purchasing a home, or planning for retirement.

- **Increasing Income**: You may need to explore new career opportunities, acquire additional skills, or start a side hustle to boost your income. Consider consulting a career coach or financial advisor for guidance.

- **Reducing Expenses**: Cut unnecessary spending and adopt cost-effective habits. This may involve downsizing your living situation, refinancing debts, or adjusting your lifestyle to match your new financial reality.

Reviewing and Updating Legal Documents

After a divorce, it is essential to review and update all financial and legal documents, including:

- **Bank Accounts and Beneficiaries**: Ensure that your bank accounts, insurance policies, and retirement accounts reflect your current situation.

- **Estate Planning**: Update your will, power of attorney, and any trust agreements.

- **Debt Responsibilities**: Clarify which debts are yours and ensure they are properly managed to avoid financial strain.

Importance of Financial Literacy and Independence

Financial literacy is key to gaining confidence and control over your money. Understanding the basics of banking, saving, investing, and credit management can prevent financial setbacks and provide security. Here are some critical areas to focus on:

- **Banking and Savings**: Maintain a separate bank account and establish an emergency fund to cover unexpected expenses.

- **Investments**: Learn about different investment options, such as stocks, bonds, and mutual funds, to grow your wealth.

- **Retirement Planning**: Contribute to a retirement fund and seek professional advice to ensure long-term financial security.

Taking Steps Toward Financial Stability

Becoming financially independent after a divorce is a journey that requires commitment and continuous learning. Here are some steps to strengthen financial independence:

- **Educate Yourself**: Take online courses, read books, or attend financial literacy workshops.

- **Consult Professionals**: A financial planner or advisor can help craft a personalized financial strategy.

- **Practice Smart Money Habits**: Automate savings, avoid unnecessary debt, and set clear financial priorities.

By taking control of your finances, you empower yourself to build a stable and independent future. Financial independence is not just about having money—it's about having the freedom to make choices that align with your goals and values.

Chapter 05

Creating a New Social Life

Reconnecting with Friends and Family

After a divorce, it is natural to reassess your social circle and reconnect with those who bring positivity and support into your life. This is a time to strengthen existing relationships, revive old friendships, and create new connections.

Strengthening Old Relationships

Divorce can be a period of transition where you realize the value of family and long-time friends. These are the people who know you well and can offer emotional support. If certain friendships faded during your marriage, now is an opportunity to reach out. A simple message or invitation for coffee can rekindle meaningful relationships. Be open and honest about your journey, but also be prepared to listen and engage in their lives as well.

Setting Boundaries and Eliminating Toxic Relationships

Just as it is essential to reconnect with positive influences, it is equally important to set boundaries with individuals who drain your energy. Divorce can be an emotionally taxing experience, and surrounding yourself with negativity can make the healing process harder. If certain friendships or family relationships are toxic—such as those who constantly bring up the past, criticize, or add stress—it may be best to distance yourself or limit contact. Focus on those who uplift and encourage you.

Expanding Your Social Circle

One of the best ways to rebuild your social life after divorce is to step outside your comfort zone and meet new people. Engaging in new activities and communities can provide fresh perspectives and friendships. Here are some ideas to consider:

Joining Social Groups

Look for groups in your community that align with your interests. Many organizations welcome newcomers, and this can be a great way to make friends who share common passions.

- **Book clubs** – A great way to engage in stimulating conversations while making new connections.

- **Community service organizations** – Volunteering for causes you care about can introduce you to like-minded people while giving back to the community.

- **Church or spiritual groups** – If faith plays a role in your life, participating in a church or faith-based group can offer emotional support and new friendships.

- **Support groups for divorced individuals** – Connecting with others who understand your journey can provide comfort and encouragement.

Pursuing Hobbies and Interests

Taking up new hobbies or revisiting old ones can help you rediscover joy and build a fulfilling social life. Some great activities include:

- **Art classes** – Painting, pottery, or drawing classes can be both therapeutic and a great way to meet new people.

- **Language classes** – Learning a new language can be intellectually stimulating and a fantastic way to connect with others who share the same goal.

- **Dance groups** – Whether it's ballroom, salsa, or line dancing, dance classes can be a fun way to socialize while staying active.

- **Fitness and outdoor activities** – Yoga, hiking, cycling, or group fitness classes provide opportunities to meet health-conscious individuals and stay physically active.

Building Confidence in Social Settings

After a divorce, it's normal to feel hesitant about putting yourself out there. However, making new friends and re-establishing a social life takes time and effort. Here are some tips:

- **Take small steps** – Start with casual meetups or group activities before diving into larger social settings.

- **Be open-minded** – Not every connection will lead to a close friendship, but every interaction can be valuable.

- **Practice self-care** – A healthy mindset and self-confidence will help you navigate social situations more comfortably.

- **Stay positive** – Focus on the opportunities that come with your new social life rather than dwelling on the past.

Rebuilding your social life after divorce is a journey, but it is also an opportunity for growth, self-discovery, and new beginnings. By reconnecting with supportive people, setting healthy boundaries, and exploring new interests, you can create a fulfilling and enriching social life.

Chapter 06

Finding Your Purpose

Divorce is not just an ending—it is also a new beginning. While the process of rebuilding can be challenging, it is also an opportunity to rediscover yourself and set new goals. This is your opportunity to let go of what no longer serves you, to dream again, and to create a future shaped entirely by your own choices. This chapter will guide you through finding your purpose, embracing your independence, and crafting a future that excites and inspires you.

Time to set New Goals

After a divorce, you may feel uncertain about what comes next. Whether you had personal aspirations before marriage or find yourself needing to create new ones, setting goals gives you direction and a renewed sense of purpose.

Career Changes, Personal Development, and Learning New Skills

Reassessing Your Career Path

If your career took a backseat during marriage or you feel unfulfilled in your current job, now is a great time to reevaluate.

Ask yourself:

- Does my career align with my passions and strengths?

- Do I want to switch fields or start my own business?

- Would additional education or training open new doors for me?

- Whether you choose to advance in your current field, return to school, or explore an entirely new industry, making a career change can be an empowering step forward.

Investing in Personal Growth

Divorce can be an opportunity for self-improvement. Consider personal development activities like:

- Attending workshops or online courses

- Reading books on self-improvement, success, and resilience

- Practicing mindfulness and emotional intelligence

- Strengthening your financial literacy

Learning New Skills

Learning doesn't stop after formal education. Expanding your skill set can increase confidence and open new opportunities. Some ideas include:

- Learning a new language

- Improving public speaking or communication skills

- Taking up writing, music, or another creative pursuit

Creating a Vision for Your Future

Once you have a general idea of where you'd like to go, it's time to create a vision for your future. Visualization can be a powerful tool in shaping your next chapter.

Journaling Your Ideal Life: A Guided Reflection

Set aside some quiet time to explore and write about the life you truly desire. Use the following prompts to guide your thoughts and spark inspiration:

Where do you want to live?

- Imagine your dream environment: Is it a cozy cabin in the woods, a beachfront villa, a vibrant city loft, or a peaceful countryside home?

- Consider the climate, culture, and community that would make you feel most alive.

- Reflect on the kind of lifestyle your ideal location supports— slow-paced and serene, or fast-moving and dynamic?

What does your perfect day look like?

- Walk through a full day in your ideal life, from the moment you wake up to when you go to bed.

- What time do you wake up? What's the first thing you do?

- What activities fill your day—creative work, meaningful conversations, nature walks, learning, or leisure?

- How do you feel throughout the day—energized, peaceful, fulfilled?

What kind of relationships and friendships do you want?

- Envision the people who surround you: What qualities do they have? How do they support and challenge you?

- What kind of romantic relationship do you desire, if any?

- What does friendship look like in your ideal life—deep, loyal connections or a wide circle of inspiring acquaintances?

- How do you show up for others, and how do they show up for you?

What personal or professional achievements matter to you?

- Think about the goals that light you up: Are they creative, intellectual, entrepreneurial, or service-oriented?

- What milestones would make you feel proud—publishing a book, starting a business, mastering a skill, making a difference?

- How do you want to grow as a person—emotionally, spiritually, physically?

- What legacy do you hope to leave behind?

Try setting SMART Goals, let's break it down

- Specific

- Measurable

- Achievable

- Relevant

- Time-bound

S – Specific: A goal should be clear and well-defined. Avoid vague statements like "I want to be better" or "I want to improve my life." Instead, identify exactly what you want to achieve.

Ask yourself: What exactly do I want to accomplish? Why is this important?

M – Measurable: Your goal should include ways to track your progress. When you can measure it, you'll know if you're moving forward and when you've reached it.

Ask yourself: How will I know when I've achieved this goal? What evidence will show my progress?

A – Achievable: Set a goal that's realistic and within your abilities, but still challenging enough to motivate you. Consider the time, resources, and effort required.

Ask yourself: Is this goal doable given my current situation? Do I have what I need to achieve it, or can I get the resources and support

I need?

R – Relevant: Your goal should align with your values, priorities, and long-term objectives. A relevant goal matters to you and contributes meaningfully to your personal growth or recovery.

Ask yourself: Does this goal fit into the bigger picture of what I want in life right now? Is it worthwhile and meaningful to me?

T – Time-Bound; Every goal needs a deadline. A time frame creates a sense of urgency and helps you stay focused and accountable.

Ask yourself: When do I want to achieve this goal? What smaller milestones can I set along the way?

Here are a few ways to set attainable goals. For example: Instead of saying, "I want to be healthier," set a goal like, "I will exercise for 30 minutes, five days a week, and track my progress for the next three months."

Creating a Vision Board

A vision board—a collection of images, quotes, and affirmations—can serve as a daily reminder of your aspirations. This simple, effective practice can help keep you motivated and focused.

Exploring New Interests

A significant part of moving forward after divorce is rediscovering joy through new experiences.

Travel: Exploring new places can be a healing and eye-opening experience. Whether it's a solo retreat, a group trip, or a local weekend getaway, travel encourages self-discovery, broadens your perspective, and allows you to step outside familiar routines.

Volunteering is another idea that can bring fulfillment while giving back and a sense of belonging. You might want to consider volunteering at:

- Local shelters, food banks, or churches.

- Schools or mentorship

- Community clean-up events

Trying New Experiences

Say Yes to life again! Say Yes to new opportunities! Whether it's signing up for a dance class, attending networking events, or trying an adventure sport, stepping outside your comfort zone isn't just about fun; it's about reclaiming your courage and reminding yourself that you're capable of growth, change, and joy.

Redefining Your Identity

After a divorce, it's natural to feel a shift in your sense of self. You may have identified primarily as a spouse, and now it's time to rediscover who you are as an individual.

Who Are You Outside of Marriage?

Reflect on what truly makes you happy. What are your values, passions, and strengths? What activities or interests light you up? The more you reconnect with your authentic self, the more you'll begin to build a life that feels whole, vibrant, and deeply yours.

Embracing Independence

Independence can be empowering, even if it feels overwhelming at first. Here are some ways to embrace it:

- Learn to enjoy solo activities like dining out, going to the movies, or traveling.

- Take control of your finances by budgeting and investing wisely.

- Build a support network of friends, mentors, and professionals who uplift and inspire you.

Creating New Traditions

Let go of old routines that no longer serve you and establish new traditions that bring joy. Celebrate milestones, create personal rituals, and honor your growth in meaningful ways.

Chapter 07

Building a Positive Mindset

The Power of Gratitude

Divorce often brings an overwhelming sense of loss, but shifting your focus to gratitude can be a transformative tool in rebuilding your life. Instead of dwelling on what's missing, gratitude helps you see what remains and what's possible. This shift in mindset can improve emotional well-being, reduce stress, and increase resilience.

How Shifting Focus from Loss to Abundance Changes Everything

Gratitude reframes your experiences. Instead of focusing on the end of your marriage, you begin to recognize the new opportunities ahead—freedom to rediscover yourself, the ability to create a life on your own terms, and the strength you've gained through challenges. Studies show that practicing gratitude leads to greater happiness, better sleep, and improved relationships. By consciously acknowledging even the smallest moments of goodness, you begin to retrain your mind to see abundance instead of loss, and in doing so, you open the door to deeper peace and genuine joy.

Daily Gratitude Practices

- **Gratitude Journal** – Write down three things you're grateful for each day, no matter how small.

- **Morning Gratitude Affirmations** – Start your day with statements like, "I am grateful for my strength," or "I am thankful for new opportunities." "I am grateful for my life." I am grateful for my health."

- **Mindful Reflection** – When feeling overwhelmed, take a deep breath and name something in the present moment you appreciate.

- **Express Gratitude to Others** – A simple "thank you" to a friend, coworker, or even yourself reinforces a positive mindset.

Overcoming Negative Thinking

Negative thoughts can feel like an endless cycle, especially post-divorce. Fear of the unknown, self-doubt, and anxiety about the future can weigh you down. However, learning to challenge these thoughts can help you regain confidence and emotional stability.

Challenging Self-Doubt and Fear of the Future

- **Reframe from focusing on negative thoughts** – Instead of thinking, "I'll never be happy again," try, "I'm learning to build happiness in a new way."

- **Focus on What You Can Control** – try to let go of the "what-ifs" and take small, actionable steps toward a fulfilling future.

- **Seek Evidence** – Ask yourself, "Is this thought absolutely true?" Most fears are based on assumptions, not facts.

- **Use Positive Affirmations** – Replace self-criticism with empowering statements like, "I am capable of building a beautiful life."

Practicing Self-Compassion and Resilience

Divorce can trigger self-blame, but self-compassion is crucial in moving forward. Treat yourself with the same kindness you would offer a friend.

1. **Try learning how to forgive yourself** – Acknowledge that mistakes and hardships are part of growth.

2. **Prioritize Self-Care** – Engage in activities that nurture your well-being, whether it's exercise, meditation, or creative hobbies.

3. **Embrace Change as Growth** – Instead of seeing challenges as setbacks, view them as opportunities for self-discovery.

Thriving, Not Just Surviving

Life after divorce isn't just about getting through the pain—it's about thriving. You have the chance to redefine what happiness means for you and embrace life with fresh enthusiasm.

Living Life with Intention and Joy

- **Set New Goals** – Whether it's traveling, learning a new skill, or starting a passion project, having something to look forward to creates excitement.

- **Embrace the Present** – Focus on savoring each moment and noticing the little things that bring joy, helping you feel more connected and grounded.

- **Surround Yourself with Positivity** – Engage with people who uplift and support you in your new chapter.

Finding Happiness in Your Own Company

One of the greatest gifts post-divorce is learning to enjoy your own company. Instead of fearing solitude, embrace it as an opportunity for self-growth.

- **Enjoy Time on Your Own** – Go to a movie, take yourself out for dinner, or take a short trip alone to gain confidence in your independence.

- **Discover Your Passions** – Reconnect with hobbies or interests that may have been set aside during your marriage. For example: sewing, crocheting, and reading.

- **Create a Personal Sanctuary** – Make your living space a reflection of your new beginning, filled with things that bring you comfort, joy, and peace.

Final Thoughts

Finding purpose after divorce is a journey, not a destination. By setting new goals, exploring fresh interests, and redefining your identity, you can build a life that reflects who you truly are. This chapter
of your life invites you to embrace change with confidence, curios-
ity, and an open heart, trusting that even after loss, there is beauty
waiting to unfold.

About the Author

Glendora Sealy is a writer, mother, and inspirational voice for anyone rebuilding their life after heartbreak. Having walked through the emotional, spiritual, and practical challenges of divorce herself, Glendora uses her story to empower others to rise, heal, and embrace the life waiting for them on the other side of pain.

Even though Glendora embraced her marriage and family for many years, she realized that with the many challenges, she no longer reflected who she was becoming. When her divorce arrived, a moment filled with uncertainty and loss, it also marked the beginning of a profound personal awakening. She discovered courage she didn't know she had, resilience she never expected to need, and a renewed relationship with God that carried her through every chapter of her transition.

Her journey led her to pursue long-held dreams, including stepping boldly into the world of **fashion design**, a passion she had quietly nurtured for years. Reclaiming her identity and following her creative calling became a vital part of her healing. Today, Glendora is committed to helping others recognize that their dreams do not end with divorce, they often begin there.

In her writing, Glendora blends faith, vulnerability, and hard-earned wisdom. She speaks to the woman who feels lost, the person starting over, and anyone seeking a fresh start without shame or fear. Her work offers compassion, clarity, and guidance for navigating life after divorce with emotional strength, spiritual grounding, and renewed hope.

When she isn't writing, Glendora enjoys designing clothing, sharing encouragement with her community, and spending meaningful time with her children, her biggest motivation, greatest blessing, and constant reminder that new beginnings are always possible. She also enjoys singing with a group in her local church.

This book is part of her mission: to help others see that they, too, can rebuild, rediscover themselves, and reclaim the life God intended for them.

A Personal Story

During the height of the divorce proceedings, my body finally began to speak in ways I could no longer ignore. The stress I had carried for so long, silently, heavily, and without rest caught up with me. I became so sick that I had to stop working completely. At the time, I didn't even realize how ill I truly was; I had pushed through everything for so long that exhaustion felt normal.

When I finally went to see my doctor, I mentioned casually that I was planning to go on a cruise, hoping a little getaway would help me reset. She looked at me with concern and gently said, *"You're not going on a cruise—you need rest.*

Her words hit me like a wave. For the first time, I understood the toll that emotional pain, constant stress, and carrying everything alone had taken on me. It was a moment of truth that humbled me and reminded me that healing is not just emotional or spiritual, but physical too.

Looking back, I realize that season taught me the importance of slowing down, truly listening to my body, and allowing myself to be cared for. It also reminded me that God often uses moments of brokenness to pull us back into His arms, where real restoration begins. My healing required me to take an entire year off from work, and during that time my personal counselor helped me navigate the emotional weight I was carrying.

That pause became a powerful turning point, a moment to reflect, to appreciate life more deeply, and to cultivate a heart of gratitude. And as my strength returned, I was blessed with the opportunity to travel, explore new places, and continue pursuing the dreams I had long set aside.